"Clang"
Went the Cymbals
An Onomatopoeia Alphabet Book

by
Dana Hall Jordan
Illustrated by
Burma Willingham

For my boys -
Ronnie, Beau & Josh
and for all those that
march to the beat of their own drum
D.H.J.

For Tracey -
who made it all happen
B.W.

Copyright 2007 by Dana Hall Jordan

All Rights reserved

Printed in the United States of America

First edition, 2008

Summary: Alphabetical sound words in a parade.

Fiction

ISBN: 978-0-9798664-0-1

Published by Capture Books - Norman, Oklahoma

Distributed by Baker & Taylor

No part of this publication may be reproduced in any manner, stored in a retrieval system, or transmitted in any manner or by any means, weather electronic, mechanical, photocopying, or in any other manner, without written permission from the publisher.

For information about custom editions, special sales and corporate purchases, please contact the publisher, Capture Books.

"Look, the parade!"

"Ahh," went the boy.

"Clang," went the cymbals in the band.

"Eek," went the mouse.

"Fizz," went the soda in his hand.

"Honk," went the horn.

"Irk," went the wheel on the float.

"Jingle," went the change.

"Kaching," went the till.

"Lick," went the blue ribbon goat.

"Oh," went the girl in the crowd.

"Plunk," went the candy.

"Quack," went the duck.

"Ruff," went the dog very loud.

"Tromp," went the feet.

"Ugh," went the boy, "where's my bear?"

"Vroom," went the go-cart.

"Waa," went the baby.

"Xss," went the ball losing air.

"Yippee," went the boy.

The End